Mia's Reflections

written by
GINGER MARKS
illustrated by Degphilip

Published by
DP Kids Press
244 5th Avenue, Suite G-200
NY, NY 10001

646-233-4366

www.DocUmeantPublishing.com

Disclaimer: This is a work of fiction. All characters appearing in this work are fictitious. Any resemblance to real persons, living or dead, is purely coincidental.

Cover & Interior Illustrator: Degphilip

Cover Design, Layout: Ginger Marks
DocUmeant Designs
www.DocUmeantDesigns.com

Library of Congress Control Number: 2018911402

ISBN13: 978-1-9378-0194-6
First Printing 2019

Printed in The United States of America

Dedication

This book is dedicated to young boys and girls everywhere.

Never let anyone tell you who you are.

Know that you are wonderful, amazing, and beautiful!

Ten year old Mia sat on her front stoop with her tabby cat, Leo, watching the people as they hurried about their daily lives.

Her parents had died in a car accident and she was sent to live with her grandmother, Ama, leaving all her friends behind.

Mia knew that soon she would have to go to a new school.
Being the "new kid" worried her.

Would she fit in? Would the kids tease her about her looks? She was sure they would.

Tall for her age, Mia had crazy, curly, red hair, and teeth too-large-for-her-mouth. She cringed at the thought of her first day in her new school.

Finally, the dreaded day arrived. Getting out of bed, Mia shuddered at the thought of what she had to face at her new school. She tried on several outfits before settling on a simple pair of jeans and her favorite t-shirt.

As Mia stepped in front of her mirror she took a deep breath. Ama had told her that the mirror was called a Cheval Mirror and was very old.

"Why do I have to be so ugly?" Mia said out loud.

Suddenly, Mia heard a soft voice that reminded her of her mother. The voice said, "Mia, you are not ugly. Oh my no! You are a very beautiful girl. Let me show you how beautiful you really are."

As Mia stared at her refection in the mirror, her image began to fade, it was filled with strange, cloudy, swirly images. When it cleared, Mia was staring at Taylor, the little boy next door. He was playing with a ball, when it started to roll into the street. Mia watched as she saw herself chasing after the ball and returning it to the toddler just before he ran out into the street after it.

This vision disappeared and slowly another one magically formed. Now, Mia saw her grandmother, Ama, preparing their supper. Standing at the kitchen stove Ama looked hot and tired.

As Mia watched, she saw herself begin to help Ama prepare the meal. She set the table without even being asked.

Next, Mia watched as an image of Leo appeared. Leo was being bullied by a neighborhood tomcat.

As soon as Mia saw her beloved cat being tormented, she rushed out and shooed the grumpy feline away. Then she picked Leo up and held him close until he calmed down and began to purr.

Slowly this vision faded away to
be replaced by a new vision. The
elderly woman, Miss B, in Mia's
building came into focus. She was
sitting in a wheelchair. Mia recalled
she had broken her hip and was still
recovering from her surgery.

As Mia looked at the image in the mirror she saw herself helping Miss B tidy up her apartment. She swept the floors, vacuumed the rugs, and carefully dusted around all the interesting knick-knacks on the tables and shelves.

Some of Miss B's shelves held some very old books.

She saw a couple that she would have liked to read, but was not brave enough to ask permission to do so.

Mia smiled at this image and how good it had made her feel to help Miss B.

Mia began thinking about what she was being shown in the mirror as the vision faded away.

When it cleared again Mia was left
looking at her own reflection.

Standing behind her in the mirror Mia saw her mother smiling back at her. In a gentle voice Mia heard her mother say, "Mia, you are a very beautiful girl. For you are not just pretty on the outside, but beautiful on the inside too."

Parent/Teacher Resources

Dear Parent/Teacher,

This simple book teaches several things. It shares the concept of true inner beauty, bullying, and peer acceptance. Also, it shows how little things matter to others and touches on life changes such as loss of a parent and moving away from friends.

To further assist you in helping your child understand the concepts presented in Mia's Reflection below you will find some helpful talking points and reading comprehension questions. Feel free to make each one easier or more difficult to suit your readers.

Additionally, I have provided you with some fun activities to share with your child/students. Talking Points

1. What was Mia worried about?

2. How would you feel if you had to leave all your friends behind and move to a strange city?

3. How would it make you feel if somebody bullied you? What could you do to help someone being bullied?

4. Why do you think Mia was uncomfortable with her looks? Have you ever felt that way?

5. How did the visions Mia's mother showed her help?

6. Can you think of ways that you could do to show your true beauty?

Reading Comprehension

1. What was Mia's grandmother's name?

2. What was Mia afraid of?

3. What was the name for the type of mirror that was in Mia's room?

4. Which character was a bully?

5. How did Mia help her neighbor, Miss B?

6. What lesson did Mia learn?

For more educational resources, coloring pages, and Mia paper doll and fashions visit:

www.MiasReflections.com

Mia's Maze

Help Mia find her way to her new school.

SOLUTION:

Mia's Vocabulary Words

Define each vocabulary word listed below, identify it's word family [(n)=noun; (v)=verb; (adj)=adjective; (av)=adverb; (s)=synonym, etc.], and memorize it's spelling.

Accident —

Ball —

Beautiful —

Bully —

Curly —

Feline —

Girl —

Grandmother —

Helper —

Mirror —

Mother —

Prepare —

Purr —

Recovery —

Red —

Reflection —

School —

Shudder —

Stoop —

Surgery —

Sweep —

Swivel —

Tall —

Tomcat —

Torment —

Vacuum —

Vision —

Wheelchair —

ANSWERS:

Accident — Ball — (n) something round

Beautiful — (adj) having the qualities of beauty

Bully — (n) a person who purposely hurts, intimidates, threatens, or ridicules another usually more vulnerable person especially repeatedly

Curly — (adj) tending to curl; having curls

Feline — (n) a animal with soft fur that includes the cats, lions, tigers, leopards, pumas, and lynxes

Girl — (n) a female child

Grandmother — (n) the mother of one's father or mother

Helper — (n) one that helps others

Mirror — (n) a smooth or polished surface (as of glass) that forms images by reflection

Mother — (n) a female parent

Prepare — (v) to make ready beforehand

Purr — (v) a low murmuring sound of a contented cat a low murmuring sound of a contented cat

Recovery — (v) to get better

Red — (adj) a color like that of blood or a ruby

Reflection — (n) the return of light or sound waves from a surface; an opinion formed or a remark made after careful thought

School — (n) a place or establishment for teaching and learning

Shudder — (v) to tremble with fear or horror or from cold

Stoop — (n) small porch or set of steps at the front entrance of a house

Surgery — (n) medical science that corrects a physical defects

Sweep — (v) to clean with a broom or brush

Swivel — (n) a device joining two parts so that one or both can move freely

Tall — (adj) having unusually great height

Tomcat — (n) a male domestic cat

Torment — (v) to cause worry, distress, or trouble

Vacuum — (n) an electrical appliance for cleaning (as floors or rugs) by suction

Vision — (n) a vivid picture created by the imagination

Wheelchair — (n) a chair with wheels used especially by sick, injured, or disabled people to get about

Mia's Vocabulary Word Search

Find the vocabulary words hidden in this puzzle.

```
c b i m t f t b m p m e y t m w o a w b
u l e y o n k o u u f l r a n n z c n v
r d n a e x t r u l r n e c r v w c j a
l w j m u h r c l i l m g m e f a i z u
y z r s e t a e g e d y r o h q s d w j
r o b r u v i e d n v p u t t t n e u z
t l o o h c s f o d r i s t o l u n c r
p e e w s x o i u e u z w o m a l t x i
f e l i n e t r p l p h p s d s r a z a
w h e e l c h a i r h t s g n m i m b h
h q g v e d r u u d p e i s a i p u r r
e i x l d e v i s i o n l p r r t d l r
t n f o e b i a e d y v b p g r n a v e
f e r e v o c e r y h x k n e o k c l d
r g s o q c h v e p s z n c n r v n d l
```

Accident	Reflection
Ball	School
Beautiful	Shudder
Bully	Stoop
Curly	Surgery
Feline	Sweep
Girl	Swivel
Grandmother	Tall
Helper	Tomcat
Mirror	Torment
Mother	Vacuum
Prepare	Vision
Purr	Wheelchair
Recovery	
Red	

```
c b i m t f t b m p m e y t m w o a w b
u l e y o n k o u u f l r a n n z c n v
r d n a e x t r u l r n e c r v w c j a
l w j m u h r c l i l m g m e f a i z u
y z r s e t a e g e d y r o h q s d w j
r o b r u v i e d n v p u t t t n e u z
t l o o h c s f o d r i s t o l u n c r
p e e w s x o i u e u z w o m a l t x i
f e l i n e t r p l p h p s d s r a z a
w h e e l c h a i r h t s g n m i m b h
h q g v e d r u u d p e i s a i p u r r
e i x l d e v i s i o n l p r r t d l r
t n f o e b i a e d y v b p g r n a v e
f e r e v o c e r y h x k n e o k c l d
r g s o q c h v e p s z n c n r v n d l
```

Mia's Cryptoquote

Use the letters of the alphabet to unlock the hidden message.

A	B	C	D	E	F	G	H	I	J	K	L	M	N	O	P	Q	R	S	T	U	V	W	X	Y	Z
U								T										A							

T _ U _   _ _ A U T _   _ _ _ _ _   _ _ _ _   T _ _
I F A L   Y L S A I G   M W K L B   H F W K   I U L

_ _ _ _ _ _ .
T X B T R L .

For more educational resources, coloring pages, and Mia paper doll and fashions visit:

www.MiasReflections.com

SOLUTION:

A	B	C	D	E	F	G	H	I	J	K	L	M	N	O	P	Q	R	S	T	U	V	W	X	Y	Z
U	S				R	Y	F	T		M	E	C					D	A	I	H		O	N	B	

T R U E   B E A U T Y   C O M E S   F R O M   T H E
I F A L   Y L S A I G   M W K L B   H F W K   I U L

I N S I D E .
T X B T R L .

www.ingramcontent.com/pod-product-compliance
Lightning Source LLC
LaVergne TN
LVHW070909080426

835513LV00004B/118